*Walt Disney Pictures Presents*

# THE LION KING

## ILLUSTRATED SONGBOOK

ISBN 0-7935-3468-2

7777 W. BLUEMOUND RD. P.O. BOX 13819 MILWAUKEE, WI 53213

© The Walt Disney Company

Copyright ©1994 by HAL LEONARD CORPORATION
International Copyright Secured    All Rights Reserved

For all works contained herein:
Unauthorized copying, arranging, adapting, recording or public performance is an infringement of copyright.
Infringers are liable under the law.

# CONTENTS

# CIRCLE OF LIFE

# CIRCLE OF LIFE

**Moderately, with an African beat**

Music *by* Elton John
Lyrics *by* Tim Rice

©1994 Wonderland Music Company, Inc. • International Copyright Secured    All Rights Reserved

*please turn the page...*

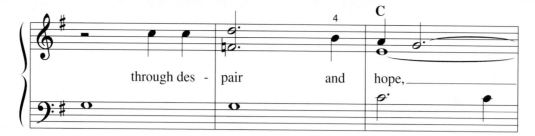

through des - pair and hope,

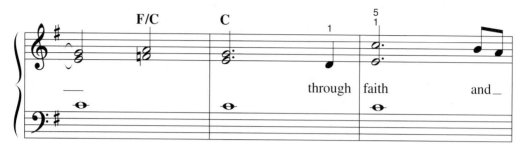

F/C    C

through faith and

Dsus    D

love,    'til we

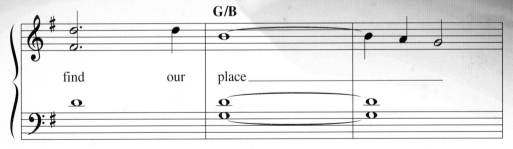

find        our        place _____

on       the       path   un -       wind    -    ing _____

*please turn the page…*

**Cm6/E♭**

in the

**G/D**                                              **Dsus**

cir - cle,                                      the

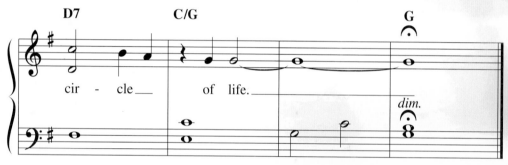

**D7**                     **C/G**                                       **G**

cir - cle          of life.                                  *dim.*

# CIRCLE OF LIFE

**Music** *by* Elton John
**Lyrics** *by* Tim Rice

From the day we arrive on the planet
And blinking, step into the sun
There's more to see than can ever be seen
More to do than can ever be done
There's far too much to take in here
More to find than can ever be found
But the sun rolling high
Through the sapphire sky
Keeps great and small on the endless round

*It's the circle of life*
*And it moves us all*
*Through despair and hope*
*Through faith and love*
*Till we find our place*
*On the path unwinding*
*In the circle*
*The circle of life*

©1994 Wonderland Music Company, Inc.
International Copyright Secured    All Rights Reserved

I JUST
CAN'T WAIT
TO BE KING

# I JUST CAN'T WAIT TO BE KING

Music *by* Elton John
Lyrics *by* Tim Rice

**Happily, with a beat**

©1994 Wonderland Music Company, Inc. • International Copyright Secured   All Rights Reserved

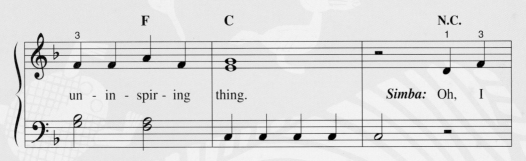

work-ing on my *(Spoken:)* roar! **Zazu:** Thus far, a rath - er

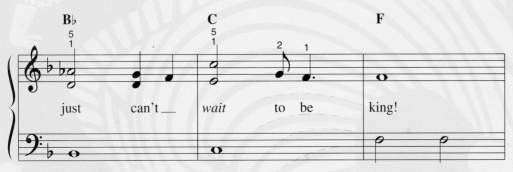

un - in - spir - ing thing. **Simba:** Oh, I

just can't ___ *wait* to be king!

**Simba:** No one say-ing, "do this," no one say-ing,
**Zazu:** *(Spoken:)* *Now when I said that I...*

*please turn the page…*

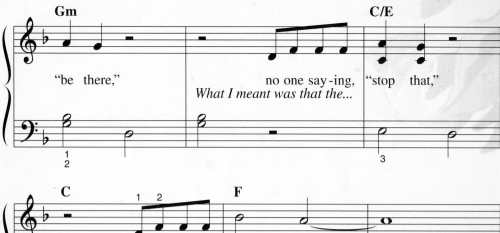

**Gm**                                                   **C/E**

"be there,"                      no one say-ing,    "stop     that,"

*What I meant was that the...*

**C**                    **F**

no one say-ing,    "see         here." _____

*But what you don't realize...*                    *Now see here!*

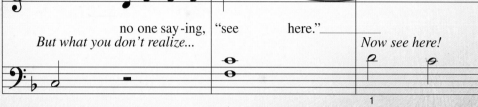

Bb     F/A     Gm     Bb     C

Free to run a - round    all ___ day,

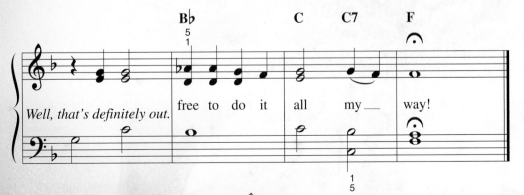

Bb     C   C7    F

*Well, that's definitely out.*   free to do it   all   my ___ way!

# I JUST CAN'T WAIT TO BE KING

Music *by* Elton John
Lyrics *by* Tim Rice

I'm gonna be a mighty king
So enemies beware!

Well, I've never seen a king of beasts
With quite so little hair

I'm gonna be the mane event
Like no king was before
I'm brushing up on looking down
I'm working on my roar

Thus far, a rather uninspiring thing

Oh, I just can't wait to be king!

No one saying do this
No one saying be there
No one saying stop that
No one saying see here
Free to run around all day
Free to do it all my way

I think it's time that you and I
Arranged a heart to heart

Kings don't need advice
From little hornbills for a start
If this is where the monarchy is headed
Count me out
Out of service, out of Africa
I wouldn't hang about
This child is getting wildly out of wing

Oh, I just can't wait to be king!

Everybody look left
Everybody look right
Everywhere you look I'm
Standing in the spotlight

Let every creature go for broke and sing
Let's hear it in the herd and on the wing
It's gonna be King Simba's finest fling

Oh, I just can't wait to be king!
Oh, I just can't wait to be king!
Oh, I just can't wait to be king!

©1994 Wonderland Music Company, Inc.
International Copyright Secured   All Rights Reserved

# Be Prepared

# Be Prepared

Music *by* Elton John
Lyrics *by* Tim Rice

©1994 Wonderland Music Company, Inc. • International Copyright Secured   All Rights Reserved

*please turn the page…*

# BE PREPARED

Music *by* Elton John
Lyrics *by* Tim Rice

I know that your powers of retention
Are as wet as a warthog's backside
But thick as you are, pay attention
My words are a matter of pride

It's clear from your vacant expressions
The lights are not all on upstairs
But we're talking kings and successions
Even you can't be caught unawares

So prepare for a chance of a lifetime
Be prepared for sensational news
A shining new era
Is tiptoeing nearer

And where do we feature?

Just listen to teacher
I know it sounds sordid
But you'll be rewarded
When at last I am given my dues!
And injustice deliciously squared
Be prepared!

It's great that we'll soon be connected
With a king who'll be all-time adored

Of course, quid pro quo, you're expected
To take certain duties on board
The future is littered with prizes
And though I'm the main addressee
The point that I must emphasize is
You won't get a sniff without me

So prepare for the coup of the century
Be prepared for the murkiest scam
(Oooooo, la la la!)
Meticulous planning
(We'll have food!)
Tenacity spanning
(Lots of food)
Decades of denial
(We repeat)
Is simply why I'll
(Endless meat)
Be king undisputed
(Aaaaaaah!)
Respected, saluted
(Aaaaaaah!)
And seen for the wonder I am
(Aaaaaaah!)

Yes, my teeth and ambitions are bared
Be prepared!

Yes, our teeth and ambitions are bared
Be prepared!

©1994 Wonderland Music Company, Inc.
International Copyright Secured   All Rights Reserved

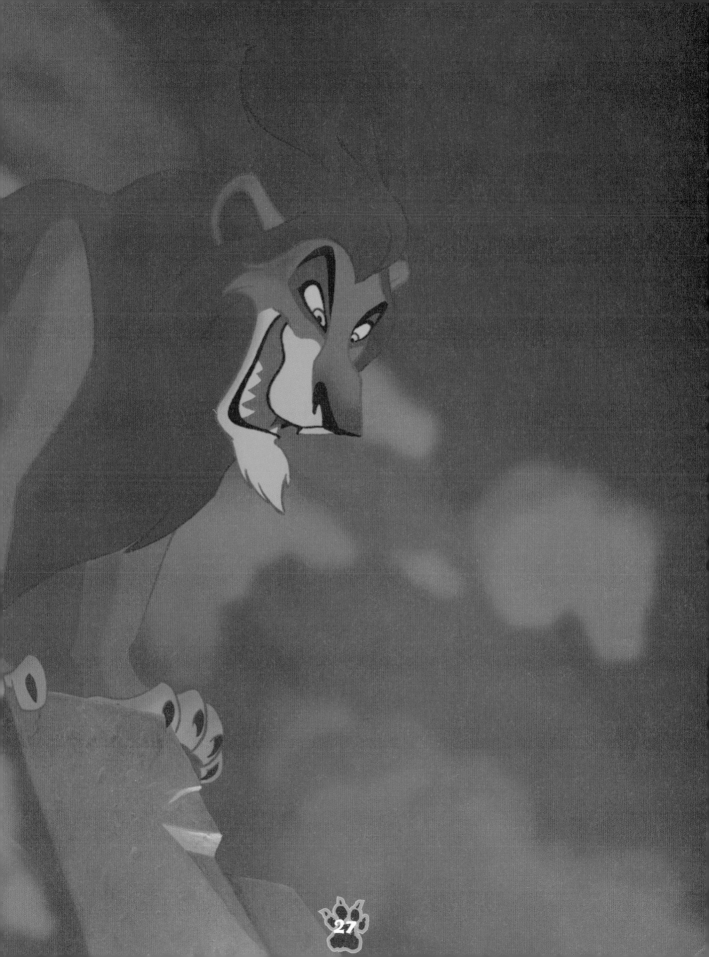

HAKUNA
MATATA

# HAKUNA MATATA

Music *by* Elton John
Lyrics *by* Tim Rice

©1994 Wonderland Music Company, Inc. • International Copyright Secured    All Rights Reserved

# HAKUNA MATATA

Music *by* Elton John
Lyrics *by* Tim Rice

Hakuna Matata!
What a wonderful phrase
Hakuna Matata!
Ain't no passing craze

It means no worries
For the rest of your days
It's our problem-free philosophy
Hakuna Matata!

When he was a young warthog
When I was a young warthog
He found his aroma lacked certain appeal
He could clear the savannah after ev'ry meal
I'm a sensitive soul though I seem thick-skinned
And it hurt that my friends never stood downwind

And, oh, the shame
Thoughta changin' my name
And I got downhearted
Ev'rytime that I…

Hakuna Matata!
What a wonderful phrase
Hakuna Matata!
Ain't no passing craze

It means no worries
For the rest of your days
It's our problem-free philosophy

Hakuna Matata!
*(Repeat)*

Hakuna…it means no worries
For the rest of your days
It's our problem-free philosophy

Hakuna Matata!
*(Repeat)*

©1994 Wonderland Music Company, Inc.
International Copyright Secured   All Rights Reserved

CAN YOU FEEL THE LOVE TONIGHT

# CAN YOU FEEL THE LOVE TONIGHT

Music *by* Elton John
Lyrics *by* Tim Rice

**Moderately slow**

*Chorus:*

*mf* Can you feel the love to-night, the peace the eve-ning brings? The world, for once, in per-fect har-mo-ny with all its liv-ing things. *dim.*

*Simba:* So *mp* man-y things to tell her, but how to make her see the truth a-bout my past? Im-pos-si-ble.

**To Coda** ⊕

©1994 Wonderland Music Company, Inc. • International Copyright Secured   All Rights Reserved

She'd turn a-way from me. *Nala:* He's hold-ing back, he's hid-ing. But

what? I can't de-cide. Why won't he be the king I know he is, the *cresc.*

king I see in - side? **D.C. al Coda** **CODA** things. *cresc.*

*f* Can you feel the love to-night? You need-n't look too

*please turn the page…*

far. *dim.*

*mf* Steal - ing through the night's un - cer -tain -ties,

love is where they are. ***Timon:*** And if he falls in love to - night,

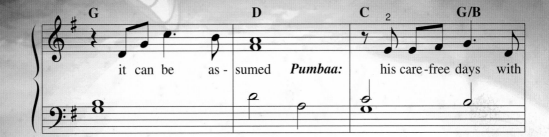

it can be as-sumed *Pumbaa:* his care-free days with

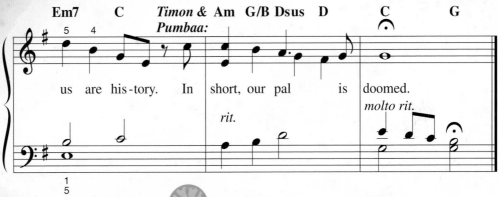

us are his-tory. In short, our pal is doomed.

# CAN YOU FEEL THE LOVE TONIGHT

**Music** *by* Elton John
**Lyrics** *by* Tim Rice

I can see what's happ'ning
And they don't have a clue
They'll fall in love and here's the bottom line
Our trio's down to two

The sweet caress of twilight
There's magic everywhere
And with all this romantic atmosphere
Disaster's in the air

*Chorus*
*Can you feel the love tonight?*
*The peace the evening brings*
*The world, for once, in perfect harmony*
*With all its living things*

So many things to tell her
But how to make her see
The truth about my past? - Impossible!
She'd turn away from me

He's holding back, he's hiding
But what, I can't decide
Why won't he be the king I know he is
The king I see inside?

*Chorus*
*Can you feel the love tonight?*
*The peace the evening brings*
*The world, for once, in perfect harmony*
*With all its living things*

*Can you feel the love tonight?*
*You needn't look too far*
*Stealing through the night's uncertainties*
*Love is where they are*

And if he falls in love tonight
It can be assumed
His carefree days with us are history
In short, our pal is doomed

❋

©1994 Wonderland Music Company, Inc.
International Copyright Secured   All Rights Reserved